A Long List of Everyday Guaranteed Rights

A Long List of Everyday Guaranteed Rights

James Sabin

A LONG LIST OF EVERYDAY GUARANTEED RIGHTS

iUniverse books may be ordered through booksellers or by contacting:

iUniverse
1663 Liberty Drive
Bloomington, IN 47403
www.iuniverse.com
1-800-Authors (1-800-288-4677)

Because of the dynamic nature of the Internet, any web addresses or links contained in this book may have changed since publication and may no longer be valid. The views expressed in this work are solely those of the author and do not necessarily reflect the views of the publisher, and the publisher hereby disclaims any responsibility for them.

Any people depicted in stock imagery provided by Thinkstock are models, and such images are being used for illustrative purposes only. Certain stock imagery © Thinkstock.

ISBN: 978-1-4917-8141-8 (sc)
ISBN: 978-1-4917-8142-5 (e)

Library of Congress Control Number: 2015918224

Print information available on the last page.

iUniverse rev. date: 03/11/2016

And More Valuable Rights

Limited help is available when undesirable people, businesses, and companies are scamming or cheating you, but you can impose your own economic sanctions against them for five years at a time. Most fraudulent people and businesses have few customers and make enormous profits, do no good for society, and quickly leave families and senior citizens in poverty. If they want to sell new products, they must stop the fraud. You are in charge.

We have the right to
- join the military, volunteer groups, and any political party of our choice;
- plant bushes—blueberry, roses, and so forth;
- enter public parks—town, city, county, state, and federal—when they are open;
- find a happy place (or a few of them);
- plead our cases;
- be entrepreneurs;
- pick our battles and win the good ones;
- adapt and stay relevant on current issues;
- be notified of all dangers and all new regulations and laws;
- have proper signage on highways—stop, slow, bump, speed limits, and so forth;
- use local library services;
- rest on the Sabbath;
- visit the sick and bring a present to a sick person;
- receive care when ill; and
- thank someone for a good deed done

No one—not even authorities—has the right to harass us during a funeral.

We have the right to
- give an apple to a teacher;
- not fear any authorities (President Franklin Delano Roosevelt);
- expect lots of good to be done for the money we spend;
- be informed of political decisions affecting our communities and protest bad political decrees affecting our municipalities;
- buy goods in respectable communities and refuse to buy items in unfriendly neighborhoods;
- transport most goods in our vehicles (except for weed);
- tow a trailer behind our vehicles (in consideration of weight limits);
- possess a first aid and/or emergency kit in our vehicles, homes, or both;
- own or rent an emergency generator for a power outage;
- go to church and praise the Lord (every week, in fact);
- celebrate Christmas and all other holidays; and
- possess books, even in our own private libraries.

Another List of Our Rights

Our quality of life depends on the rights we have. When we lose some rights, we do fewer good projects, families suffer, and civilization declines. When senior citizens are cheated or lose rights, they usually cannot recover. It's usually permanent damage.

We have the right to
- learn the arts (music, painting, languages, and so forth) and/ or skills; and
- access good quality, safe food and clean, nontoxic water.

Growing vegetables is not a right in all communities but should be in case of national disaster, major climate change, war, long-term traffic problems, and so forth.

We also have the right to
- relief from the harsh weather elements;
- fair and honest business dealings;
- freedom from police abuse and brutality; and
- anything that is legal (but safe and within reason).

The five basic survival needs are oxygen, water, food, shelter, and sleep. We have a right to these.

We have the right to ethics in finance and a fair and honest court system. We have the right to
- remain silent;
- be free from corruption;
- videotape police (with some restrictions);

- be protected against false, misleading, deceptive, and fraudulent schemes; hazardous products; and an unhealthy environment;
- know of recalled products and our consumer rights;
- call for redress (receive settlements for shoddy goods and services and misrepresentation); and
- be informed and be heard (consumer feedback).

We have the right to satisfaction of basic needs: adequate food, goods, services, clothing, public utilities, shelter, health care, education, water, and sanitation. We have the right to use the bathroom. It is not a privilege. Nature says we have to go.

We have the right to
- complain to the government and assemble;
- request a speedy and public trial, bail, and impartial jury;
- be informed of what crime we are accused of and why;
- be confronted with the witness against us;
- call a witness in our favor; and
- be protected from being a witness against ourselves, having the authorities' conduct be protected from unreasonable searches and seizures, and having private property taken without just compensation.

Another List of Your Rights

We have the right to an adequate standard of living, necessary social services, and security in the event of unemployment, sickness, disability, widowhood, old age, or other livelihood in circumstances beyond our control. Motherhood and children are entitled to special care and assistance. All children, whether born in or out of wedlock, shall enjoy the same protection.

We have the right to be free from fear at all times and display the American flag and the MIA and/or POW flag. We have the right to continuous improvement of living conditions and adequate food, clothing, and housing. Adequate standard of living is a social right.

We have the right to a fair and honest credit score. We have the right to
- question and correct dishonest credit scores without any exceptions;
- have only fair and honest financial transactions with no exceptions;
- obtain a receipt for every financial transaction;
- receive an honest answer for every question; and
- request a third party examine our loans and credit scores, which is sometimes necessary.

We have the right to fair, honest, and reasonable loan payments, including the last payment.

We have the right to
- bake an apple pie;
- carry a phone and a camera, which may not be allowed in some places;

- plant a tree;
- access the Internet; and
- not be sleep deprived.

We have the right to
- a retirement plan;
- survival tools and items;
- some personal time; and
- personal hygiene.

We have the right to
- visit friends and neighbors;
- protect our possessions;
- maintain a safe and secure home, which is sometimes expensive;
- have local authorities provide security protection;
- attend local events; and
- pen a book.

We have the right to continue our education, even go to college. Many courses are free. We have the right to
- attend local town board meetings;
- know all local laws and regulations; and
- know names of all politicians affecting our lives, Republican or Democrat.

We have the right for local authorities to not target or constantly harass us.

And Another Long List of Rights

There is a need for more aggressive and tougher penalties for consumer rights violations for everyone, mainly people on fixed incomes and three times over for senior citizens, to stop abuses and injustices.

We have the right to
- possess labor-saving machines, tools, equipment, and electric devices, which are usually not free;
- maintain our homes, yards, and gardens;
- access public services, including fishing ponds, beaches, swimming pools, and public bathrooms;
- sit down when sick or tired (mainly senior citizens);
- access all public businesses and buildings, unless prohibited to all;
- question all wrongdoing by businesses or government agencies; and
- query any financial statement for accuracy and receive an answer.

We have the right to carefully read and question all billing statements we receive. Often mistakes can be found. We also have the right to
- well-maintained and safe transportation, which may be expensive;
- a bank and savings account; and
- a reasonable final payment when paying off loans or business accounts.

We have the right to

- live in any town, city, county, or state; and
- be treated with respect and be given the benefit of doubt by all business and government agencies.

We have the right to a free lawyer if we cannot afford one and for the police or courts to let us off with a warning if it is a first-time minor offense, a right which is usually denied.

We have the right to stay away from unfriendly towns and businesses and refuse to buy new products if treated unfairly.

We have the right to live in dignity in retirement. We have the right to reasonable health costs, health care, and benefits. We have the right to caregiver services for senior citizens.

We have the right to

- obtain warnings about scams, abuse, rip-offs, injustices, bank levies, and any seizures in advance;
- request a second opinion any time we want, which is often wise to do;
- call for help in emergencies and access emergency services— police, fire department, and ambulance—and helpful neighbors; and
- refuse any or all services not wanted.

We have the right to a retirement hobby. We have the right to extra rights and privileges for senior citizens.

We have the right to

- never be left stranded anywhere;
- always be told the truth about anything and everything;
- live in harmony at home and anywhere we go;
- develop agreements with businesses and government agencies; and
- travel by public transportation, like air, rail, bus, or taxi.

We have the right to fair and just tax on income, property, sales, and so forth. We have the right to shade on a hot day and adequate clothing, boots, and gloves on a cold day.

We have the right to
- have visitors anytime we want;
- celebrate holidays;
- demand more rights;
- keep personal papers and possessions secure with a safe or lock, protecting them from a warrant or burglars;
- access communication, phone, TV, Internet, newspaper, pigeon, and so forth;
- maintain a personal library;
- continue our education; and
- try a new career at any age.

Another Long List of Rights

All government agencies are compelled to protect our rights and provide services. We have the right to
- be treated as people;
- indulge in recreation such as fishing, hunting, and swimming with proper permits (limited);
- say no, which may often be challenged; and
- obtain disability aids, such as wheelchairs, walkers, ramps, and so forth.

All government agencies and businesses must do no harm and do lots of good in every transaction. We have the right to buy new products and refuse all new merchandise if we are treated badly. The average consumer is in charge of the economy. There are many millions of us.

We have the right to live normal lives. We must be safe and do no harm. We have the right to never be scammed, cheated, stolen from, or deceived by anyone. We have the right to privacy—for example, while taking a bath or shower and getting dressed. We have the right to communicate via telephone or Internet, and we can have TV and contact with outside world.

We have the right to
- provide for home and family;
- visit sick family members and incarcerated persons;
- celebrate all holidays we choose;
- enjoy nature and all its beauty;
- access heat on a cold day or evening;

- inherit property; and
- be protected from excessive taxes (Magna Carta).

We have the right to solidarity—that is, formation of consumer/citizen groups to ensure justice for consumers. We have the right to involvement or action so that consumers can assert themselves to get a fair deal.

We have freedom from unwarranted infringement by governments and private organizations. We have freedom to participate in civil and political life without discrimination or repression. We have civil rights—for the well-being of our physical and mental integrity, life, and safety.

We have the right to
- assemble, defend ourselves, and vote;
- be protected from cybercrime;
- not associate with unethical people who have questionable behavior;
- demand better consumer rights protection;
- socialize with church members, friends, community groups, senior citizen groups, and so forth;
- travel south to escape cold winters; and
- drive our vehicles of choice, if they are legal for the highway.

All people have the right of self-determination. By virtue of that right, they freely determine their political status and pursue their economic, social, and cultural development (International Covenant of Human Rights [ICHR]). No one shall be imprisoned merely on the grounds of inability to fulfill contractual obligations (ICHR).

We have the right to enjoy all human rights and fundamental freedoms.

Arrests and Jobs Theory

I believe the massive number of arrests for the past four decades and high unemployment are connected. There is a competition for jobs and a much fiercer rivalry for leadership roles, decision-making positions, offices of authority, law enforcement, and extra-high salaries with benefits and perks. These jobs are wanted for the next generation of the decision makers, a few people who want to run the country. There are very few elite job openings each year.

Also wanted for the next generation of the elite is the ability to go to the best colleges to train for these jobs. There are common, hard, low-paying jobs for us and decision-making, high-paying jobs for the children of the elite. The job applications of the authority in the public and private sector are very much protected, shielding the next chosen few to run the country.

This scam started many years earlier to knock out the competition by arrests. A person with a criminal record is not considered for employment for the better jobs. He or she is knocked out of contention. Millions of people are refused employment because of criminal records.

It is illegal to target people, giving criminal records for little or no reason. So the police and courts want to hand out all possible charges to make this plan work for millions of young people. Almost no competition is left to get into good colleges and the jobs required to be in charge of our lives. This is why we now have so many low-quality department heads. In some towns and city blocks, every person between the ages of sixteen and thirty has a criminal record. It was overdone, and many people cannot even get an entry-level job.

Many young people are wrongfully convicted on trumped-up charges and eventually take plea bargains. This scam is the root of the angry riots we have today, and most of our poverty cannot be corrected until the next generation is born today. If not corrected, it will be the end of our country, the loss of our nation.

A company does not build and hire people in a community where all the present and future employees have criminal records. These arrests and job problems exist in all fifty states, and independent groups and Congress must research them.

Listen to the people at the riots. We want jobs, answers, and true justice. Feel free to explore, examine, discuss, and research this theory any way you wish. I believe this to be true and unproven, but if it looks like a duck, walks like a duck, and quacks like a duck, it likely is a duck.

Civil Asset Forfeiture

The civil asset forfeiture law is terrifying and has a dark side. It needs to be outlawed and repealed from coast to coast. It allows the IRS, DEA, police, Border Patrol, and others to seize cash and property without proof of criminal behavior. It can be based on policing for profit with no warrant needed. They only need to suspect or assume it is tied to drug money. Oftentimes only false complaints are needed for the search and seizure.

The people in charge of this dog-and-pony show will not or cannot read the Constitution. If real criminals have their assets seized, they are left with their loaded guns and can replace the assets in a matter of hours. But innocent people have long-term permanent damages. They are unable to meet payroll, restock shelves, and pay overhead business expenses. And they are unable to get it back. Bad leaders of foreign governments operate on this theory. Police abuses seize millions of dollars from motorists, and they are not charged with crimes or due process of the law.

The dysfunctional civil forfeiture law is legal, but it destroys the country. Starting up a small business requires some cash, but the risk is not worth it if it can be seized on a false complaint. Many entrepreneurs and innovators are hesitant to move forward with their ventures because of this cruel law. Some outdoor-sports stores have some products that will bite unwanted fingers that are taking money or property, which may be useful here. Do not get stopped on the way to pay cash for a car.

Also, why should companies return from overseas when all cash and property is seized without the due process guaranteed by the Constitution? Also, federal privacy laws prohibit the IRS from commenting on any taxpayer's case. So getting any money or property back is dead in the water. We the people.

Consumer Rights and Consumer Loans

We have the right to fair and honest financial dealings. There seems to be serious problems with some. Payday loans have many complaints. Credit cards also have their share of grievances. More serious are auto and thirty-year loans. I found the worst is the "daily accrued interest loan." I had one, and after signing the loan, I was forbidden to pay monthly at the local branch office. The payment had to be received on only a certain day each month. I had to send the check to another state to arrive on that day, which is impossible to do.

I was never late, but after six years, I owed more than I started with. I lost many thousands of dollars on that legal deal. I wish to propose that the government agencies examine all consumer loans to reform them. Follow up on the complaints, correct the problem loans again, and punish the businesses and people doing it. Do not punish the consumer with late charges and fees, essentially depriving good families of much-needed funds.

The companies make 99 percent of their profit from sales of new goods. The customers do just fine with good used products and alternative services until they get a better deal. The government agencies reserve the right to make the rules and laws but do not seem to protect us from the unethical and seedy big businesspeople. We need a better way to know how to separate the good ones from the bad before we sign a thirty-year loan.

When I was young, we would keep the good companies near and dear to the family for life, but this cannot be done today. If we had all respectable loans to apply for, the economy would be back to normal much sooner. If the unethical business people were removed, there would be more employment for honest people and more money for necessary expenses.

Remember that we have the right to fair and honest financial dealings. Demand them.

Customs and Traditions

It all started with the hunter-gatherer caveman people. There were no customs or traditions thousands of years ago. They were uncivilized, hungry, uneducated, and usually very bad-tempered people. It was just brutal basic survival, hunting woolly mammoths, mastodons, and many other animals with very dangerous weapons. It was a big job to cook a woolly mammoth. There were no rules, regulations, laws, or taxes. It was very unsafe every time they left the cave. There was very little communication among the cave dwellers.

If one cave family had several young male sons and another had several daughters, it was unsafe for one family to visit the other cave to get acquainted. It was too dangerous to go there without great possible harm. It was usually too dangerous for bartering.

There were very hazardous weapons in the caves. It took several thousands of years to become half-civilized and later have tribal law, unwritten code, and some social rule. It occurred over centuries of trial and error.

Moses and the Ten Commandments is believed to be the first record of written law. The Commandments made great strides in social order and made it safer to move about the community to do daily business and visiting. This was the beginning of law, customs, and traditions—rules and laws for everyone to live by in a civilized society—to be brought out of a primitive, savage state. We then became a more polite, cultured, educated, courteous, and advanced people.

The next milestone was the Constitution and Bill of Rights. We now have the ability to protect all of the good in society. Going back in time is not for humanity. It took many thousands of years to advance to the humanity we have today. Let's not go back in time.

If we all follow the rules of human rights, consumer rights, and all other rights, the best centuries are ahead of us. This history teaches us that all things are possible once we all have our rights.

Let's not go back to being cave dwellers. There are no woolly mammoths left to eat. Now is the time to go forth and build beautiful and wonderful things. We the people!

Economic Recovery Rights

This page is about how to preserve our economy. There are many parts to economic recovery. I will cover one important part that is overlooked. I mentioned earlier about some major Wall Street, mortgage, credit card, and other companies cheating consumers. Often the customer will protest an inaccurate billing statement. Unable to win, he or she will complain to authorities. But he or she still cannot win. The bad, undesirable company will continue to cheat people. Why?

I believe we may have a solution. Cheating millions of people every day has a major cost to people, families, and the country. We must ask citizen consumer protection agencies to find names of true owners, lobbyists, board members, consultants, and a complete list of shareholders of each company that is being investigated for wrongdoing. Some bad company workers may be related to government officials. Very often government authorities or immediate family members are board members of bad companies. Almost all government authorities hold shares in Wall Street companies.

Often when you read the names of board members and shareholders and compare them with political officials, you will find the answer. It creates a serious conflict of interest. When a high-level politician is a major shareholder in a crooked company, the problem will never get better. There is profit in crime. Millions of dollars go missing every day this way. It causes serious harm to every area of society.

There should be a law that no politician, judge, lawyer, or government employee can invest in any company or stock market if there is even one unresolved complaint or serious penalty awaiting. This will stop the amoral company leaders from preying on people.

It will force them to read the ethics manual; follow all laws, the Constitution, and the Bill of Rights; be good neighbors; and read this book.

If still no problem is resolved, we can go to the Internet, YouTube, or TV stations. We can make many phone calls to the bad company, publish names and phone numbers, file lawsuits, join class action suits, refuse to buy new products, and send them a bill for our wasted time.

Again no animals or feathered friends were harmed while writing this page. Perhaps some feelings were wounded, but we need several consumer rights groups with lots of authority and a set of handcuffs to work on this important problem. This is my opinion, and I am sticking to it.

We have the right to check if all areas of the financial industry meet state, national, and international standards. Thank you for your interest.

Long List of Your Guaranteed Rights

We have the right to
- privacy and freedom from abuse, mistreatment, and neglect;
- oxygen to breathe; and
- freedom from physical and chemical restraints.

We have the right to
- be treated with dignity;
- communicate freely;
- participate in resident and family groups;
- be accommodated for medical, physical, psychological, and social needs;
- take part in the review of one's care plan and be informed in advance about changes in care; and
- obtain an abortion (with some limitations).

Men and women—black, white, or any other color—are all equal. We have the right to equal pay for everyone and at least a minimum wage. We have the freedom of
- press and speech;
- opinion and expression;
- privacy (with some restrictions); and
- movement/travel.

We have the right to demand or refuse medical care. But this treatment may not be free. We have the right to refuse drug testing (with some restrictions). We have the right to own property, procure adequate housing, and bear arms. We have rights concerning children, including work conditions, abuse, and pornography.

We have the right to
- marry and have families;
- obtain free public education;
- start our own businesses;
- advance economically and socially; and
- elect not to do so.

We are innocent until proven guilty. We have the right to an attorney. He or she can be present during questioning by police or officials. We have the right to a fair trial by a jury of our peers. We have freedom from cruel and unusual punishment.

We have the right to a vote, political freedom (who to vote for), an opinion that doesn't agree with our government, and a say in the laws that are made. We have the right to protest and question.

And More Important Rights

Some laws concerning lethal force and brutality do not meet international standards. We have the right to check if the following meet international standards: lethal and/or brutal force by police, civil forfeiture, no-knock laws, property seizure without being charged, and IRS money and property seizures. We have the right to learn international standards on all laws.

We have the right to
- buy, rent, and/or lease property;
- sell or loan unneeded personal property;
- buy a motor home and travel for weeks or years;
- give a friendly wave;
- demand public services that taxes paid for;
- join a political party;
- learn all of world and American history, from ancient to early to modern;
- learn the stock market and buy shares in it;
- live in harmony with family, friends, all citizens, and authorities;
- meet obligations; and
- join unions.

We have the right to good quality lives. We have freedom from scams, cheats, and unethical people.

We have the right to
- not be assumed to be guilty;
- look up the content of any law when needed;

- sue when falsely charged; and
- guarantee authorities are always right.

No mistakes are allowed in this zero-tolerance world. We have the right to ask for leniency.

We have the right to
- not suffer from need, hunger, heat, shelter, medical, and so forth;
- provide for ourselves when possible;
- communicate with others;
- sleep in complete safety;
- eat and drink three times per day; and
- buy daily newspapers and magazines.

We have the right for authorities to question us without fear. We have the right to receive the benefit of the doubt from authorities and all businesses.

We have the right to a family reunion. We have the right to retain records on all transactions.

John F. Kennedy Message to Congress Protecting the Consumer Interest

1. The right to safety—to be protected against goods hazardous to health or life.
2. The right to be informed—to be protected against dishonest, fraudulent, deceitful, misleading labeling and to be given the facts to make informed choices.
3. The right to choose—to be able to select from a range of products and services at competitive prices with an assurance of satisfactory quality and service at fair prices.
4. The right to heard—to have consumer interests represented in the making of government policy.
5. The right to consumer education—to gain knowledge and skills of fair and honest dealings, to be aware of basic consumer rights and how to act on them.
6. The right to a healthy environment—to have a safe environment suitable for present and future generations.
7. The right to redress—to receive fair settlement for claims, including shoddy goods, misrepresentation, and unjust dealings.
8. Fair and honest business dealings—financial protection of savings and future purchases.
9. Formation of consumer/citizen groups who work together to have influence and strength to have attention to protect consumer interest.

***

I would like to add that it is wise to try to always have a witness in this more aggressive world. Nearly all businesses, parking lots, and other places have security cameras. You can use them as a witness when you have conversations and conduct business. You can use them for personal safety. You can have your own security camera nearby. Many bad things happen to good people, and it's smart to have a witness whenever possible.

Stay in full view of the camera. Free security is hard to beat.

We're Not in Kansas Anymore

I have visited Kansas twice while on vacation. I loved the state, with its very kind people and rolling hills. It reminds me of Mayberry. I also like the phrase about Kansas because it brings attention to a possible problem or potential solution.

This chapter is about consumer rights, information about which is available at www.USA.gov/Consumer. President Obama approved this book titled *Consumer Action Handbook*. Every person in America is a consumer and is guaranteed consumer protection by law, but it is seldom enforced. It seems to always to favor big business and government. I have struggled for many decades to have consumer rights, and I was disappointed. Many companies have no ethics. Thousands of consumer laws on the books are seldom enforced. Having consumer laws better enforced would result in fewer home foreclosures, auto repossessions, and loss of monthly income by those undesirable people. I no longer have Verizon Wireless or Asset Recovery Solutions, LLC 877-253-3543. It was paid in full twice, and they still demand a third payment, which is very bad.

Bad consumer protection laws leave low credit scores. About half have serious errors. It forces us to have to pay very high interest rates. We are unable to correct errors. It's a disaster for the economy, a very serious problem.

When in doubt, the customer should get the benefit of the doubt. We need the consumer financial rights so that we can have a better future, safer homes, education, tools to work with, home maintenance, needed items, and decent retirement. All business and government depend on consumer spending. Without it, most would collapse. I no longer have Citi Mortgage.

Today, it mostly lets the buyer beware, but it is a major problem if we sign contracts. I wish to no longer finance with Ford Credit. A public outcry or class action may help solve the problem. They cannot win against millions of unhappy people.

Better enforced consumer rights and honest credit scores would quickly improve the economy. Only people of good character should be allowed in business and the government in charge of our lives. I no longer have One Main Financial. You may know some questionable companies to be aware of but need more solutions. We all need to find them so that we can stop losing so much money to them.

Once we find the solution, the economy will start to boom again. We should not have to fear big businesses and their accounting offices. We pay our tax dollars to the government to provide the service of consumer rights for us average people. Once the average citizens and families have some prosperity, they are better behaved and cause fewer problems, so we must stop cheaters and fraudsters from draining their monthly income.

Often many businesses and government agencies can be difficult to deal with. Once they take unfair advantage of us, you can refuse to buy only the new products and refuse financing for five years at a time—the heart of our economy. Many thousands of people do it now until we get all of our consumer rights.

Once we get more respect, keep us happier. We will have a better economy. The average citizen is in charge of the economy but has no voice. I write; you decide. Thank you.

The World Only Turns in One Direction

The world and everything on it only turns in one direction, in an orderly fashion, and if anyone or something wants to travel in a different direction, it will cause major chaos. The Constitution and Bill of Rights also turn only in one direction, like the best well-oiled machine in the world when read and followed properly. Once they are tampered with and diluted, many undesirable things can happen.

The economy has been below normal for many years. Most of our younger generation has a bleak future because of too many police records, lack of skills, and loss of some Bill of Rights and constitutional rights. Big and small companies are constantly scamming them.

When the future is too bleak too long, many young people will find drastic ways to make their future better by joining a half-human radical military in another country. A few hundred have already gone. It's time now to correct it before we have a mass exodus. Do not rob the next generation so that the haves can get more. Our military may have to fight the have-nots.

The government is a guardian of our Constitution and Bill of Rights. If we put the Constitution and Bill of Rights back in its original form, it will fix most of the world's problems overnight. The Constitution and Bill of Rights gives all level of government, businesses, and citizens the common ground rules of law to work with in harmony with great respect for country and elected officials.

Never force anyone to have a zero future. Good leaders always make things better for everyone; bad leaders leave us in tears. It's very simple. This is my opinion and open to debate.

You Also Have These Rights

We have the right to
- a decent quality of life;
- good health, safety, and well-being; and
- solar products and lighting.

We have the right to
- sell, loan, buy, and/or rent products;
- do anything that is safe, healthy, and legal;
- be investors, entrepreneurs, and/or innovators;
- demand public trust in our elected officials;
- cook for ourselves and others; and
- keep food and drinks cold.

We have the right to equal opportunity for a good future. We have the right to
- shop for the best deals on products and ask for senior discounts;
- travel to warmer climates for winter;
- purchase boats and/or ATV vehicles;
- own lawn and garden tools and our own equipment for DIY projects;
- possess watches and clocks;
- sleep in a bed; and
- buy cleaning supplies.

We have the right to
- be American citizens;
- celebrate the Christmas holiday, along with all festivals on the American calendar; and
- keep all of our rights forever and regain past lost rights.

We have the right to
- learn needed skills for future use;
- put up "no trespassing" signs;
- ask others to attend with invitation-only cards; and
- send (unless unwanted) and receive phone calls, texts, and e-mails without problems.

We have the right to truth in government and business. We also have the right to
- expect more rights as senior citizens;
- demand protection from civil asset forfeiture and no-knock entries;
- go to all of our doctor appointments;
- obtain portable survival kits; and
- live alone or in a family unit.

We also have the right to wear the clothing of our choice, including shoes or sandals. But formal wear does usually have restrictions. We have the right to travel on vacation to the beach and national parks. This may all be seasonal.

We have the right to study the following state, national, and international rights: disability, civil, financial, and personal.

We have the right to drive any automobile model and color and purchase automobile insurance, which is recommended. We have the right to "I Love the Constitution" bumper stickers on our cars.

We have the right to a safe, pleasant, attractive home. We have the right to decorate the inside of our homes any way we wish. We have the right to a small workshop and office. We have the right to a storage space and/or shed, keeping tools in there for repairs.

Senior citizens have the right to a life without turmoil with lots of comforts for their final years. They have the right to
- access disability aids, walkers, and wheelchairs;

- learn all of their senior citizen rights—state, national, and international; and
- join senior citizen groups and agencies.

Senior citizens have the right to be treated with lots of respect by everyone and never be regarded in a cruel or neglected way. They have the right to have most wishes and needs be met. They have the right to pen a journal of their thoughts and words of wisdom. They have a right to their last will and testament.

Senior citizens have the right to always have the benefit of doubt from all companies and agencies. They have the right to never be cheated, scammed, and/or mistreated or incur penalties three times. They have the right to have visitors any time they choose.

We have the right to family pictures. Some have four generations in them. We have the right to alternative ways to do most things.

We have the right to say "Good morning" and "Thank you and good night."

The American's Creed by William Tyler Page

I believe in the United States of America as a government of the people, by the people, for the people; whose just powers are derived from the consent of the governed, a democracy in a republic, a sovereign Nation of many sovereign States; a perfect union, one and inseparable; established upon those principles of freedom, equality, justice, and humanity for which American patriots sacrificed their lives and fortunes.

I therefore believe it is my duty to my country to love it, to support its Constitution, to obey its laws, to respect its flag, and to defend it against all enemies.

—Written 1917, accepted by the United States House of Representatives on April 3, 1918

Preamble

Whereas recognition of the inherent dignity and of the equal and inalienable rights of all members of the human family is the foundation of freedom, justice and peace in the world,

Whereas disregard and contempt for human rights have resulted in barbarous acts which have outraged the conscience of mankind, and the advent of a world in which human beings shall enjoy freedom of speech and belief and freedom from fear and want has been proclaimed as the highest aspiration of the common people,

Whereas it is essential, if man is not to be compelled to have recourse, as a last resort, to rebellion against tyranny and oppression, that human rights should be protected by the rule of law,

Whereas it is essential to promote the development of friendly relations between nations,

Whereas the peoples of the United Nations have in the Charter reaffirmed their faith in fundamental human rights, in the dignity and worth of the human person and in the equal rights of men and women and have determined to promote social progress and better standards of life in larger freedom,

Whereas Member States have pledged themselves to achieve, in co-operation with the United Nations, the promotion of universal respect for and observance of human rights and fundamental freedoms,

Whereas a common understanding of these rights and freedoms is of the greatest importance for the full realization of this pledge,

Now, Therefore THE GENERAL ASSEMBLY proclaims THIS UNIVERSAL DECLARATION OF HUMAN RIGHTS as a common standard of achievement for all peoples and all nations, to the end that every individual and every organ of society, keeping this Declaration constantly in mind, shall strive by teaching and education to promote respect for these rights and freedoms and by progressive measures, national and international, to secure their universal and effective recognition and observance, both among the peoples of Member States themselves and among the peoples of territories under their jurisdiction.

Article 1.

- All human beings are born free and equal in dignity and rights. They are endowed with reason and conscience and should act towards one another in a spirit of brotherhood.

Article 2.

- Everyone is entitled to all the rights and freedoms set forth in this Declaration, without distinction of any kind, such as race, colour, sex, language, religion, political or other opinion, national or social origin, property, birth or other status. Furthermore, no distinction shall be made on the basis of the political, jurisdictional or international status of the country or territory to which a person belongs, whether it be independent, trust, non-self-governing or under any other limitation of sovereignty.

Article 3.

- Everyone has the right to life, liberty and security of person.

Article 4.

- No one shall be held in slavery or servitude; slavery and the slave trade shall be prohibited in all their forms.

Article 5.

- No one shall be subjected to torture or to cruel, inhuman or degrading treatment or punishment.

Article 6.

- Everyone has the right to recognition everywhere as a person before the law.

Article 7.

- All are equal before the law and are entitled without any discrimination to equal protection of the law. All are entitled to equal protection against any discrimination in violation of this Declaration and against any incitement to such discrimination.

Article 8.

- Everyone has the right to an effective remedy by the competent national tribunals for acts violating the fundamental rights granted him by the constitution or by law.

Article 9.

- No one shall be subjected to arbitrary arrest, detention or exile.

Article 10.

- Everyone is entitled in full equality to a fair and public hearing by an independent and impartial tribunal, in the determination of his rights and obligations and of any criminal charge against him.

Article 11.

- (1) Everyone charged with a penal offence has the right to be presumed innocent until proved guilty according to law in a public trial at which he has had all the guarantees necessary for his defence.
- (2) No one shall be held guilty of any penal offence on account of any act or omission which did not constitute a penal offence, under national or international law, at the

time when it was committed. Nor shall a heavier penalty be imposed than the one that was applicable at the time the penal offence was committed.

Article 12.

- No one shall be subjected to arbitrary interference with his privacy, family, home or correspondence, nor to attacks upon his honour and reputation. Everyone has the right to the protection of the law against such interference or attacks.

Article 13.

- (1) Everyone has the right to freedom of movement and residence within the borders of each state.
- (2) Everyone has the right to leave any country, including his own, and to return to his country.

Article 14.

- (1) Everyone has the right to seek and to enjoy in other countries asylum from persecution.
- (2) This right may not be invoked in the case of prosecutions genuinely arising from non-political crimes or from acts contrary to the purposes and principles of the United Nations.

Article 15.

- (1) Everyone has the right to a nationality.
- (2) No one shall be arbitrarily deprived of his nationality nor denied the right to change his nationality.

Article 16.

- (1) Men and women of full age, without any limitation due to race, nationality or religion, have the right to marry and to found a family. They are entitled to equal rights as to marriage, during marriage and at its dissolution.

- (2) Marriage shall be entered into only with the free and full consent of the intending spouses.
- (3) The family is the natural and fundamental group unit of society and is entitled to protection by society and the State.

Article 17.

- (1) Everyone has the right to own property alone as well as in association with others.
- (2) No one shall be arbitrarily deprived of his property.

Article 18.

- Everyone has the right to freedom of thought, conscience and religion; this right includes freedom to change his religion or belief, and freedom, either alone or in community with others and in public or private, to manifest his religion or belief in teaching, practice, worship and observance.

Article 19.

- Everyone has the right to freedom of opinion and expression; this right includes freedom to hold opinions without interference and to seek, receive and impart information and ideas through any media and regardless of frontiers.

Article 20.

- (1) Everyone has the right to freedom of peaceful assembly and association.
- (2) No one may be compelled to belong to an association.

Article 21.

- (1) Everyone has the right to take part in the government of his country, directly or through freely chosen representatives.
- (2) Everyone has the right of equal access to public service in his country.

- (3) The will of the people shall be the basis of the authority of government; this will shall be expressed in periodic and genuine elections which shall be by universal and equal suffrage and shall be held by secret vote or by equivalent free voting procedures.

Article 22.

- Everyone, as a member of society, has the right to social security and is entitled to realization, through national effort and international co-operation and in accordance with the organization and resources of each State, of the economic, social and cultural rights indispensable for his dignity and the free development of his personality.

Article 23.

- (1) Everyone has the right to work, to free choice of employment, to just and favourable conditions of work and to protection against unemployment.
- (2) Everyone, without any discrimination, has the right to equal pay for equal work.
- (3) Everyone who works has the right to just and favourable remuneration ensuring for himself and his family an existence worthy of human dignity, and supplemented, if necessary, by other means of social protection.
- (4) Everyone has the right to form and to join trade unions for the protection of his interests.

Article 24.

- Everyone has the right to rest and leisure, including reasonable limitation of working hours and periodic holidays with pay.

Article 25.

- (1) Everyone has the right to a standard of living adequate for the health and well-being of himself and of his family, including food, clothing, housing and medical care and necessary social services, and the right to security in the event of unemployment, sickness, disability, widowhood, old age or other lack of livelihood in circumstances beyond his control.
- (2) Motherhood and childhood are entitled to special care and assistance. All children, whether born in or out of wedlock, shall enjoy the same social protection.

Article 26.

- (1) Everyone has the right to education. Education shall be free, at least in the elementary and fundamental stages. Elementary education shall be compulsory. Technical and professional education shall be made generally available and higher education shall be equally accessible to all on the basis of merit.
- (2) Education shall be directed to the full development of the human personality and to the strengthening of respect for human rights and fundamental freedoms. It shall promote understanding, tolerance and friendship among all nations, racial or religious groups, and shall further the activities of the United Nations for the maintenance of peace.
- (3) Parents have a prior right to choose the kind of education that shall be given to their children.

Article 27.

- (1) Everyone has the right freely to participate in the cultural life of the community, to enjoy the arts and to share in scientific advancement and its benefits.

- (2) Everyone has the right to the protection of the moral and material interests resulting from any scientific, literary or artistic production of which he is the author.

Article 28.

- Everyone is entitled to a social and international order in which the rights and freedoms set forth in this Declaration can be fully realized.

Article 29.

- (1) Everyone has duties to the community in which alone the free and full development of his personality is possible.
- (2) In the exercise of his rights and freedoms, everyone shall be subject only to such limitations as are determined by law solely for the purpose of securing due recognition and respect for the rights and freedoms of others and of meeting the just requirements of morality, public order and the general welfare in a democratic society.
- (3) These rights and freedoms may in no case be exercised contrary to the purposes and principles of the United Nations.

Article 30.

- Nothing in this Declaration may be interpreted as implying for any State, group or person any right to engage in any activity or to perform any act aimed at the destruction of any of the rights and freedoms set forth herein.

Thirty-one Basic Human Rights

1. We are all born free and equal.
   a. We all have our thoughts and ideas.
2. Don't discriminate.
3. The right to life
   a. This also includes safety.
4. No slavery
   a. This means past, present, and future.
5. No torture
   a. No one has the right to hurt or torture you.
6. We have rights no matter where we go.
   a. We all have the same right to use the law.
7. We're all equal before the law.
   a. The law protects us; it must treat us fairly.
8. Our human rights are protected by law.
   a. We can ask the courts to help us when treated unfairly
9. No unfair detainment
10. The right to a (fair) trial
11. We're always innocent till proven guilty.
12. The right to privacy
    a. No one is allowed into our homes without permission or warrant.
13. Freedom to move
    a. We may travel as we wish.
14. The right to seek a safe place to live
    a. If we are too frightened to live somewhere, we have the right to live elsewhere.
15. Right to a nationality
    a. You have the right to belong to a country.

16. Marriage and family
    a. All persons of legal age can marry and have a family.
17. The right to your own things
    a. We have the right to own things or share them. These things are not to be taken away.
18. Freedom of thought
    a. We have the right to have beliefs and religion.
19. Freedom of expression
    a. We have freedom to say what we think, have our own minds, and share ideas with others.
20. The right to public assembly
    a. We have freedom to meet where we like, meet our friends, and work together to defend our rights.
21. The right to democracy
    a. We have the right to take part in our government and choose our leaders.
22. Social security
    a. We have the right to affordable housing, medicine education, child care, enough money to live on, and medical care when old or sick.
23. Workers' rights
    a. All of legal age have the right to a job, fair wages, and ability to join a trade union.
24. The right to play
    a. We all have the right to rest from work and relax.
25. Food and shelter for all
    a. We have the right to a bed and some food. We all have the right to a good life. All people, including the elderly, unemployed, and disabled, have the right to be cared for.
26. The right to education
    a. Education is a right, not a privilege. Primary school is free.
27. Copyright
28. A free and fair world

29. Responsibility
    a. Freedoms extend to other people. We need to protect their rights too.
30. Men and women have the same rights when married as when they are separated.
31. No one can take away your human rights.
    a. Nobody can take away these rights and freedoms from us.

Loss of Rights and Results

It's a very sad day if we ever lose all of our rights in America. Even in the twenty-first century, many countries in the Middle East and Africa, once prosperous, have no functional government, basic rights, and public safety. Sometimes they have no right to life. Now they are living in the Stone Age. The Stone Age and twenty-first century are still closely related. Without any rights, we will return to the Stone Age.

Each year we are losing a little more Constitutional and Bill of Rights privileges with justified shooting of unarmed citizens and civil seizure of assets. We are losing the glue that holds everything together. There is much more discontent among average citizens. Some laws are legal but not right and must be reexamined. When the discontent reaches the point of no return, we will lose our government and never want it back. It's a complete loss of respect.

Our country is quickly losing its ability to connect the dots and tell the truth. It is quickly losing ancient history and citizens without criminal records. We must do a complete study of once-prosperous countries around the world that are now living in the Stone Age without any rights so that we do not find ourselves in the same situation.

We must have a major world campaign to promote more basic men's, women's, and children's rights. We have many brilliant people among our citizens and should allow their input for solutions for the future of our country. Unhappy people never build good things.

World history—Stone Age, Bronze Age, Iron Age, Industrial Age, and others—has the answers, but do not believe rewritten history. Just connect the dots.

Thank you, and have a nice day.

Major Threats to Our Rights

In my opinion, the greatest threat is the no-knock law when a group of police enters any home or business in the middle of the night while people are sleeping unannounced and raid it with a warrant that may be shown later. There are seventy to eighty thousand no-knock raids in the United States yearly. Many go horribly wrong and should be stopped. There seems to be no oversight or controls as they use military equipment and tactics on American citizens.

The Supreme Court refuses to hear the case to vote if it is legal. The no-knock law will likely be expanded into something much more sinister. There should be a panel of citizens, including older veterans, for oversight of the program. The older veterans will remember the no-knock laws used in Europe during World War II.

The fourth amendment of the constitution states,

> The right of the people to be secure in their persons, houses, papers, and effects, against unreasonable searches and seizures, shall not be violated, and no warrants shall issue, but upon probable cause, supported by oath or affirmation, and particularly describing the place to be searched, and the persons or things to be seized.

The police have a finger to ring the doorbell. They should use that appendage to show the warrant first and guarantee not to raid the wrong house or harm innocent people. There are 670,000 police in America. There is no shortage of manpower, and there is no need for military equipment.

The no-knock law should be put on hold until we get a final decision from the nine justices on the Supreme Court to decide if is legal and what limits it has. The program is very scary if it is to be expanded. Nothing is safe anymore. Anyone or anything can be seized or searched. Sometimes it's the wrong house. Often false leads and incorrect information will lead to disaster.

I believe the program is morally and legally wrong. The government has an obligation to do us lots of good in everything it does. We seem to have lost our neighborhood security. Some of us may have to fend for ourselves at night. With many protests on the Internet and the mainstream media, all of the fourth amendment violations can be corrected. It's very sad.

More Guaranteed Rights

We have the right to all
- God-given, natural, and constitutional rights;
- children, family, and senior citizen rights; and
- voting and property rights.

We have the right to
- assistance during an emergency and disaster;
- all consumer rights and protection from all forms of fraud;
- all civil rights;
- product safety and services from the Financial Protection Bureau;
- primary and higher education; and
- Social Security, Medicare, and Medicaid (subject to age and financial restrictions).

We have the right to access renewable energy. We have the right to
- a bank account;
- insurance coverage, specifically medical, property, unemployment, and/or life;
- tenant rights, if needed; and
- Internet access.

We have the right to access the Truth in Lending Act and invest in our future. We have the right to
- an attorney;
- health care, specifically clinics, doctors, hospitals, and nursing care;

- trustworthy credit reports; and
- honest interest on loans with no scams.

We have the right to access small claims court in order to file a claim against any wrongdoing and dispute any transgression. We have the right to write a will. There's no need to hurry on this one.

We have the right to choose utility providers. It's wise to check list of complaints first to protect yourself. We have the right to know who the bad companies are before we sign. The Better Business Bureau (BBB) may be a good start. We have the right to shop for the best loan interest deals before signing.

No animals or feathered friends were harmed while writing this book.

Much Needed Rights

We have the right to
- own an air-conditioner, mechanical and electrical tools, and lawn and garden equipment;
- keep a gun (with lots of restrictions) and knife; and
- own a drone (with few restrictions).

We have the right to pick who our friends are. We have the right to go fishing, but we must follow all regulations. We have the right to play golf, baseball, basketball, and other sports.

We have the right to
- be proud Americans;
- deal only with people of good character and refuse to talk to or deal with very rude people;
- purchase health and life insurance for self and family;
- obtain property coverage, along with fire, wind, and so forth;
- compile a first aid/emergency kit (recommended);
- go to weddings, graduations, and funerals;
- call an attorney anytime and make at least one phone call; and
- sue in court to keep all of our rights.

We have the right to be people of good character and do everything to the best of our ability. This is recommended. We have the right to live normal lives and in peace, not constant turmoil.

We have the right to be frugal and save money for a rainy day. We have the right to enter sweepstakes and contests. We have the right to self-sustainable living and renewable home energy, especially for heating and cooling. We have the right to solar lights, lamps, and so forth. We have the right to own solar panels. They're portable and extremely useful. We have the right to air-circulating fans for hot weather and the ability to sit outside on nice days.

We have the right to preserve food at home and keep a windowsill garden. We have the right to a refrigerator and/or freezer for food storage. We have the right to collect rare coins, books, and jewelry. It's best to stay with small items.

Mystery of the Credit Scores

This is my opinion of how the credit scores operate. I have a personal interest in it. My wife lost her credit at age twenty-three, regained it at age sixty-two, and died at age sixty-four. Now the credit bureau is doing the same to me. I am a senior citizen and cannot wait that many years. They usually refuse to correct disputed charges, leaving it on the credit report for years. Are you next?

I believe the credit score problem is more of an illusion to maximize profits. First there are three credit score agencies, undesirable bad companies, respectable good businesses, selective good scores for few, and discriminatory bad scores for the rest of us. It needs to be investigated and corrected every year. Having honest credit scores is our guaranteed right. Many millions of extra funds are made daily, and someone is getting a massive payoff to let it happen. But who?

The scores appear to be massaged and manipulated and do no good. Some accounts take years and have to be paid two or three times to be adjusted. The credit score agencies find it cheaper to not fix a problem than to fix it. Are the credit score agencies untouchable?

The people in charge of the scores determine who will succeed and who will live in poverty. The purpose of keeping the scores low is to make extra large profits with most of it going to undesirable companies and showing profits for the good businesses.

As years go by, the greedy people take more free money from the outrageous interest charges, causing permanent harm to our economy. The country is in serious decline from it. This possible extortion of our economy without watchdogs may be the permanent end of our economy.

The selective lowering of scores on purpose is a loss of several millions of dollars daily going to those undesirable questionable people. Someone must fix the problem. There is no one true credit score. Some lenders add their own different formulas and forget to use some good. The credit score people will listen to public outcry as consumers refuse to buy new products. They fear being called before Congress numerous times, a class action lawsuit, and a major fear of being taken out of the office in handcuffs. Now they will be agreeable to correct the problem.

Also when there are millions of dollars taken fraudulently every day, who is getting the massive payoff to let it happen? The credit score people need a shorter leash. You also have the right to write a book about it. This is my opinion. Ignore it if you disagree. I needed my fifteen minutes.

Tampering with credit scores to keep them low is illegal, and the persons responsible should be severely punished. Low credit score means instant poverty. I write; you decide. Thank you.

Rights v. Privileges

Rights cannot be taken from you; privileges can and are often removed. Privileges are often just as important as rights. You have a right to own a vehicle, but it is a privilege to drive it. Many people must drive as part or all of their living. Rights and privileges often go hand in hand with each other, as with vehicles.

We must complain loudly and often when our rights or privileges are taken away so that we can have social progress. Some agencies quickly take away privileges to punish people, but it also hurts the economy when it's done widely and often. If we all lost our privileges to drive vehicles, the economy would likely drop to zero and may never recover. We need the trucks and autos to move goods to and from the markets. The government does not get taxes on goods that stay on the shelf forever. It has to move.

A permit to build is a privilege and sometimes takes years to get, but it uses a lot of goods and products and greatly helps the local economy. We still need vehicles to move products from point A to B. Rights and privileges are tied together again. It's almost impossible to do one without the other. We need more studies on the effects of privileges on society. They can be taken away without any reason and not be returned.

People are also voters. If a privilege is denied, they are required to give you a satisfactory answer: who, what, where, when, and why. And keep asking again and again. To get things done, we need results. Privileges we have need to be protected as much as rights. You do can most of it yourself in your spare time. Demand all of them.

Big companies and agencies have massive daily overhead expenses. They will eventually give in to keep consumers, but all rights and privileges first and accurate financial figures second. This will produce a healthy economy, and we will not have to die in poverty.

Poverty stops all forms of progress. Families and individuals come first. Consumers are not morons. They are our friends and families—smart and well educated. And there are lots of us. The consumers are in charge of the economy, and they must and will be respected.

No company is better than a bad company. Life is not all ice cream sundaes.